Pathways
to God

Series Preface

The volumes in NCP's "7 x 4" series offer a meditation a day for four weeks, a bite of food for thought, a reflection that lets a reader ponder the spiritual significance of each and every day. Small enough to slip into a purse or coat pocket, these books fit easily into everyday routines.

Pathways to God

Four Weeks on Faith, Hope and Charity

Robert F. Morneau

New City Press
Hyde Park, New York

Published in the United States by New City Press
202 Cardinal Rd., Hyde Park, NY 12538
www.newcitypress.com
©2008 New City Press

Cover design by Durva Correia

Library of Congress Cataloging-in-Publication Data:

Morneau, Robert F., 1938-
    Pathways to God : four weeks on faith, hope, and charity / Robert F.
Morneau.
        p. cm.
    Includes bibliographical references.
    ISBN 978-1-56548-286-9 (pbk. : alk. paper) 1. Spiritual life--
Chirstianity. 2. Faith--Meditations. 3. Hope--Meditations. 4. Charirty--
Meditations. I. Title.

BV4501.3.M6735 2008
248.4--dc22   2007028634

Printed in the United States of America

Contents

one
The Vision of Faith

two
Boundless Hope

three
God Is Love

four
Path of Perfection

Foreword

Down through the ages, humankind has struggled with belief and unbelief. Human reason takes us only so far in grasping the truth. Human language falters before mystery. Besides reason, another path lies open before us: the path of faith. Without evidence, we trust in the word and witness of another. Without evidence, we come to interior convictions that offer us meaning and direction. And when both reason and faith are given their proper due within the same soul, much blessedness and peace will be there too.

Down through the ages, humankind has struggled with hope. In glancing into the unknown future, what are we to expect? Is there something beyond suffering and death? Is hope simply an attempt to escape from the harshness of reality? Or, is hope and confidence in God an anchor that gives us energy and enthusiasm to build up the Kingdom of God? In a culture that deals with despair and depression, we need to re-experience the hope which trusts that the promises God has made to us will come true.

Again, every generation struggles not only with faith and hope, but also with the virtue of charity. Saint Paul told us quite clearly that one day faith and hope will vanish, but love will remain. God is love. We, made in the image and likeness of this God, are called to be lovers, people of concern and respect, of responsibility and generosity. Not to live out the virtue of love is to miss out on life itself.

The methodology of this small volume is to present reflections on faith, hope, and charity from a variety of sources. Each week will begin with a song/hymn that invites us to proclaim our faith in each of these theological virtues. Then we will listen to poets, to essayists/novelists/philosophers, and to theologians. The first week will deal with faith, the second with hope, and the third and fourth with charity (week three — love of God; week four — love of neighbor). Each day will end with a question and short prayer.

In baptism, we were called to a virtuous life. May this book help each of us to answer that call more completely.

The Vision
of Faith

A Song of Faith

Songs carry our theology. Before we turn to the intellectuals and their gift of articulating the mysteries of our faith, we do well to turn to the psalmists as they sing for us about God's plan of salvation. In hymns, the whole person is drawn in to experience various aspects of God's life within and around us. As one pundit put it, you will never hear anyone leaving church humming a homily, but they will be humming the hymns. In the Divine Office, the following hymn is presented as the person praying enters into morning prayer. It is a magnificent summary of our faith — our faith in the Trinity, our faith in the Incarnation, our faith in the gift of the Holy Spirit, our faith in eternal life. Hum this hymn and reflect upon its words and your faith will grow by leaps and bounds.

On this day, the first of days,
God the Father's name we praise:
Who, creation's Lord and spring,
Did the world from darkness bring.

On this day the eternal Son
Over death his triumph won;

*On this day the Spirit came
With his gifts of living flame.*

*Father, who didst fashion man
Godlike in thy loving plan,
Fill us with that love divine,
And conform our wills to thine.*

*Word made flesh, all hail to thee!
Thou from sin hast set us free;
And with thee we die and rise
Unto God in sacrifice.*

*Holy Spirit, you impart
Gifts of love to every heart;
Give us light and grace, we pray,
Fill our hearts this holy day.*

*God, the blessed Three in One,
May thy holy will be done;
In thy word our souls are free,
And we rest this day with thee.*

(Le Mans Breviary)

Question: What does this hymn tell you about the mystery of God? What is your favorite stanza?

Prayer: Lord Jesus, may we sing joyfully of our faith. Help us to experience more deeply the mystery of your love and mercy manifest in the Trinity and Incarnation.

2 George Herbert's Vision of Faith

One of the deepest hungers of the human heart is to love and be loved. George Herbert, the 17th century Anglican priest and poet, prays that he be taught to know God's love — both the love God has for him and the grace of love to be received and passed on to others. The last stanza, spoken at dawn, is a prayer of faith. All we need in terms of revelation is but a single sunbeam which, if understood, discloses both creation and the Creator. All this is prayed in an atmosphere of a providential God who woos us and offers total availability. The human heart must be truly amazing for God to respond in this way. This God of presence never abandons us, and it is impossible to awaken outside the divine milieu. Surely, then, we should make a covenant each morning as to how we shall spend the day and, come night, count the sunbeams encountered.

My morning soul? Far different from my evening one. At dawn, my soul is all poverty, empty of busyness and fear. It's naked, simple and uncomplicated. It's vulnerable to many lights and to honest appraisal. It's lonely and hurries off to fill the void.

Matins

I cannot ope mine eyes,
But thou are ready there to catch
My morning soul and sacrifice:
Then we must needs for that day make a match.

My God, what is a heart?
Silver, or gold, or precious stone,
Or star, or rainbow, or a part
Of all these things, or all of them in one?

My God, what is a heart,
That thou shouldst it so eye and woo,
Pouring upon it all thy art,
As if that thou hadst nothing else to do?

Indeed man's whole estate
Amounts (and richly) to serve thee:
He did not heav'n and earth create,
Yet studies them, not him by whom they be.

Teach me thy love to know;
That this new light which now I see,
May both the work and the workman show:
Then by a sunbeam I will climb to thee.

(George Herbert)

Question: What helps you to increase your awareness of God's presence?

Prayer: Lord Jesus, you are with us at all times — with the coming of the morning light, in the darkness of evenings, in our midnight fears. May we stay always in your presence.

3 Jessica Powers & Faith

My mother died several weeks before Jessica Powers, the Carmelite poet, in 1988. At both funeral liturgies, I recited "The Homecoming." Christian faith is based on the Resurrection, that sin and death have been overcome by the Lord's redemptive love and life. Upon death we return to (fall back into) the source of our being. Upon death we are welcomed home like the prodigal son, and a banquet awaits us. And even though sin, with its concomitant shame and guilt, is part of our history, we have confidence in God's longing for us and his infinite mercy. So much glory here in God's radiant love!

Rembrandt's painting of the prodigal son's return to his father is well known. The aged father, half blind and not quite so regal, embraces his repentant son with tenderness and mercy. What a homecoming even though not appreciated by all (the elder son). God, too, has a robe, a ring, music, and a meal awaiting us who turn from darkness toward the light, from death to life. And we need not wait — our salvation is now!

The Homecoming

The spirit, newly freed from earth,
is all amazed at the surprise
of her belonging: suddenly
as native to eternity
to see herself, to realize
the heritage that lets her be
at home where all this glory lies.

By naught foretold could she have guessed
such welcome home: the robe, the ring,
music and endless banqueting,
these people hers; this place of rest
known, as of long remembering
herself a child of God and pressed
with warm endearments to His breast.

(Jessica Powers)

Question: What is your attitude toward death?

Prayer: Lord Jesus, deepen our faith in the risen life. May we experience the death of our loved ones as it truly is, a homecoming. And when we die, share with us the robe, the ring, and the music of your love.

4 Faith: A Vision of Reality

When Saint Paul, then Saul, was persecuting the members of the early Church, he experienced the mystery of Christ on that road to Damascus. This was no daydream; this was no myth that would help explain the meaning of life. No, it was a revelation and vision about the way things are. By injuring those early Christians, Paul was harming the very Mystical Body of Christ. Now, gifted with faith, Paul would venture forth and share this new vision of reality with everyone who would listen.

> *The moral of all this is an old one; that religion is revelation. In other words, it is a vision, and a vision received by faith; but it is a vision of reality. The faith consists in a conviction of its reality. That, for example, is the difference between a vision and a daydream. And that is the difference between religion and mythology.*
>
> *(G. K. Chesterton)*

Only now, in the midst of everything that man may think or experience, in the midst of all that is known as "world," rises a point that does not belong to the world; a place into which one may step; a room one may enter; a power on which one may lean; a love to which one may give oneself. This is reality, different from the reality of the world, more real than the world. Faith is the act of seizing this reality, of building one's life on it, of becoming a part of it.

(Romano Guardini)

Question: What is your vision of reality; what meaning do you assign to life?

Prayer: Lord Jesus, open our minds and hearts to your revelation. Help us to see reality for what it is and to embrace your revelation as truth.

5 Learning to Believe

Flannery O'Connor (1925–1964) was a woman of hope and faith. She understood well the trials that post-modern people deal with: radical doubt, skepticism, despair. All of her writings and correspondence in some way dealt with faith. The doctrines of creation, redemption, and sanctification permeated her works and her personal life. She died at age thirty-nine of lupus, but not before leaving the world a testimony of faith at once shocking and marvelous. She felt that in a culture where people are hard-of-hearing you have to shout, when they cannot see, you draw large, distorted pictures. In the end, faith would win the day and resurrection would trump death and sin.

> Do you know the Hopkins-Bridges correspondence? Bridges wrote Hopkins at one point and asked him how he could possibly learn to believe, expecting, I suppose, a physical answer. Hopkins only said, "Give alms." What people don't realize is how much religion costs. They think faith is a big electric

blanket, when of course it is the cross. It is much harder to believe than not to believe. If you feel you can't believe, you must at least do this: keep an open mind. Keep it open toward faith, keep wanting it, keep asking for it, and leave the rest to God.

Faith is a gift, but the will has a great deal to do with it. The loss of it is basically a failure of appetite, assisted by sterile intellect. Some people, when they lose their faith in Christ, substitute a swollen faith in themselves.

About the only way we know whether we believe or not is by what we do.
                                                (Flannery O'Connor)

Question: Is there any way of truly knowing whether we have faith?

Prayer: Lord Jesus, you revealed to the disciples and to us the extravagance of your Father's love and mercy. Deepen our faith. Help us to put into practice the values of your Kingdom. By so doing, we demonstrate and witness to our belief in you.

6 A Faith Awakened

Most of us are not changed just by being given knowledge. But when we are exposed to individuals and communities that love and live the truth, then we are truly challenged to look at our lives and, quite often, make significant adjustments if not an outright conversion. As the saying goes, faith is more caught than taught. Living biblical values brings about major conversions.

Doctrinal instruction by itself is incapable of awakening faith in the hearer, only doctrine in which the teacher himself believes. It is when truth is loved and lived that it awakens faith. It is the faith of your mother, or your teacher, or your friend, or some other person around you, which has awakened your own. At first, without knowing it, you have lived with them in their faith; then your own faith arose, became definite, and finally found the strength to stand upright. Just as a candle is lit by contact with the flame of another candle, so faith enkindles faith.

Behind the impenetrable obscurity which envelops the beginning of faith there lies an even profounder mystery: faith is the work of God. All those efforts of thought, those instances of perception, those emotions caused by religious values, those encounters with the saints, are the materials in which the true artisan, God, accomplishes his work. Becoming a believer is the effect of a divine action which touches, transforms, illumines, draws us, while remaining shrouded in the mystery of grace. No psychological analysis, no logical reasoning can penetrate there.

(Romano Guardini)

Question: Who are the people who awakened your faith? What were the circumstances of that awakening?

Prayer: Lord Jesus, keep the flame of faith alive in our hearts. Grant us the courage to light the candles of others, sharing with them the faith so graciously given to us.

7 Faith's Transformative Power

Faith is so rich in its many levels of meaning. There is an intellectual component of revealed truth; there is an affective dimension of a loving relationship between Creator and creature; there is an imperative layer wherein we put into practice what God is asking us to do. Faith is illusive in the sense that it contains so many values: trust and confidence, love and affection, conviction and commitment. If it is not easy to define, it is easy to spot in action. Faith-filled people transform our world.

Ideally, faith should take root in the deepest level of the human personality. It should transform believers from within, orienting them in a new way toward God as their creator, savior, and last end. Faith should make a person doctrinally orthodox, trustful, obedient, and socially committed. It should go out to God as one who is to be believed, trusted, obeyed, and loved. I see no reason why faith, without loss of its identity, could not have all these dimensions. Where one or another of these characteristics is lacking, faith must be judged to be mutilated or imperfect.

Faith is seen as a welcoming response to God's self-offer, trustful reliance on his saving help, obedient submission to his sovereign lordship, and assent to his revealing word.
(Avery Dulles)

Question: What is your working description of faith? What is the one quality of faith that is most significant in your life at this time?

Prayer: Lord Jesus, continue to teach us how to believe. Our faith is often weak and weary, our minds so clouded and dense. Send your Spirit of faith into this dark world and grace us with the courage to believe and to do your will.

Boundless Hope

And Grace Will Lead Me Home

Grace is so many things: participation in divine life; the experience of God's love and mercy; the gift of the Holy Spirit. However we describe it, it is truly amazing. Grace is unmerited and undeserved, yet there it is, available to all who ask. Herein is our hope: that, despite our unworthiness and infidelity, God's love continues to be offered to us. How can we keep from singing?

One of the most powerful moments of grace is hope. The philosopher defines hope as "an arduous search for a future good of some kind that is realistically possible but not yet visible" (William Lynch). The poet Wordsworth tells us: "But indignation works where hope is not." The essayist Emerson comments: "We judge a man's wisdom by his hope." But it is the musician who helps get hope into our hearts. Once there, it wants to remain.

Amazing Grace

Amazing grace! how sweet the sound
That saved a wretch like me!
I once was lost, but now am found,
Was blind but now I see.
'Twas grace that taught my heart to fear,
And grace my fears relieved;
How precious did that grace appear
The hour I first believed!
The Lord has promised good to me,
His word my hope secures;
He will my shield and portion be
As long as life endures.
Through many dangers, toils, and snares,
I have already come;
'Tis grace has brought me safe thus far,
And grace will lead me home.
When we've been there ten thousand years,
Bright shining as the sun,
We've no less days to sing God's praise
Than when we'd first begun.

(John Newton)

Question: What are some of the amazing graces in your life? Share some of those life-giving moments with a friend.

Prayer: Lord Jesus, we ask for the grace of hope. You are true to your promises and we rely on your word. Keep depression and despair far from our hearts. Instill in us the grace to face the future with great expectations.

2 Sweet Hopes

Edgar Allan Poe (1809–1849) was not known for his religiosity. However, he was moved deeply after hearing about a devotion called the "Angelus," a three-minute prayer that recalled the Annunciation story of Gabriel appearing to Mary. In that story the angel asked Mary if she would be willing to become the mother of Jesus. For centuries, Catholics prayed this devotion early in the morning, then at noon, again in the evening. Poe, in reflecting upon this prayer form, wrote the following verse, a poem that looked toward the future with sweet hopes.

Hymn

At morn — at noon — at twilight dim
— Maria! thou hast heard my hymn!
In joy and woe — in good and ill —
Mother of God, be with me still!
When the Hours flew brightly by,
And not a cloud obscured the sky,
My soul, lest it should truant be,
Thy grace did guide to thine and thee;

Now, when storms of Fate o'ercast
Darkly my Present and my Past,
Let my Future radiant shine
With sweet hopes of thee and thine!
(Edgar Allan Poe)

Question: How do you deal with your three time zones: the past, the present, the future?

In looking toward the future, what are your sweet hopes?

Prayer: Lord Jesus, the regrets of the past and the troubles of the present can overwhelm us. May we look to the future, our union with you and the communion of saints, with joyful expectations, that is, with sweet hopes.

3 In May ...

It is difficult to hope in the dead of winter. The land is fallow, the sun is shy, the trees are barren. Cold winds chill the soul and the darkness instills fears. Unless God sends us angels, we can despair.

But, just as God sent an angel to the barren Sarah bringing her good news of life, so too we can hope that good news will come unexpectedly our way. Life and love do spring eternal in the human heart and our dreams and hopes will not be thwarted. Apple trees and old women and young men all know this deep in the soul.

Another Sarah
for Christopher Smart

When winter was half over
God sent three angels to the apple-tree
Who said to her
"Be glad, you little rack
Of empty sticks,
Because you have been chosen.

In May you will become
A wave of living sweetness
A nation of white petals
A dynasty of apples."

(Anne Porter)

Question: Over the years, how many angels came into your life? What news did they bring?

Prayer: Lord Jesus, our poverty is immense. Unless you give us life and hope, we shall be lost. Take care of every apple-tree; take care of us all that we might bear fruit, fruit that will last unto eternal life.

4 Hope: The Courage to Experience Life

Depression and despair paralyze. These moods cause a diminishment of energy and an introversion that short-circuits life. Without hope, individuals tend to become inactive and do not engage in writing or reading, in sharing or caring, in plunging into human experience. By contrast, people who see the future filled with possibilities strive to realize their potential and contribute something to the common good.

> *People without hope not only don't write novels, but what is more to the point, they don't read them. They don't take long looks at anything, because they lack the courage. The way to despair is to refuse to have any kind of experience, and the novel, of course, is a way to have experience.*
>
> *(Flannery O'Connor)*

Question: What do you take long looks at? How is this "contemplative attention" related to hope?

Prayer: Lord Jesus, may we experience our presence and have the courage to hope in your promises. Do not let us or our friends despair.

The Choice: Hope or Despair

In his poem "Fire and Ice," Robert Frost holds out to us the choice of how the world might end: in the fire of anger through some nuclear holocaust or through the ice we see in the bottom of Dante's *Inferno* where sinners are locked in icy isolation. Daily we are presented with choices: "To be or not to be" as Shakespeare describes, to live or to die as Moses puts before his people, to hope or despair as Eliade reflects on here:

> But I feared a Soviet occupation, even a temporary one. One always fears a giant neighbor. Giants can be admired only from a distance. But the choice had to be made: despair or hope. And I am always against despair of that kind, political or historical despair. So I chose hope. I told myself that it was simply one more ordeal that had to be gone through — we are only too familiar with the ordeals of history — we Romanians, Yugoslavs, Bulgarians, all of us — because our existence has always lain between empires.
>
> (Mircea Eliade)

Question: What are the giant forces around you that demand a choice of either hope or despair? How can you face ordeal after ordeal without despairing?

Prayer: Lord Jesus, in the desert and in the garden, you faced the ordeals of temptations and death. Be with us in our struggles for we are weak and vulnerable. May we hope always in your sustaining presence.

A Total Hope 6

Just as peace can be piecemeal, so too our hope. Sometimes our hope might be limited to expectations that are less than universal, focused on this world, and centered on the present moment. But a full, complete hope embraces all people, future life, and a life that never ends. As we grow in our Christian life, our hope too must expand to be more and more inclusive.

> My goal will be to commend a full Christian hope — a total hope. By this is understood a hope that envisions a universal renewal and restoration, yet one which also finds room for the fulfillment of each individual whom God has called into existence; a hope that would be this-worldly and evolutionary in the sense that everything that we do now in the way of building up truth, love, peace and community can be understood as co-operating with God's purposes for his creation, yet that would also be other-worldly and revolutionary in the sense that the goal would be understood as a transformed mode of existence beyond what

we can visualize from our present situation; a hope that would be future yet also present in the sense that its full shape lies ahead and is not yet wholly discernible, yet also present in the sense that here and now through our communion with God and our fellowship with one another in the communion of saints we can have at least a glimpse or foretaste of eternal life.

(John Macquarrie)

Question: In what sense can our hope be less than total? What is the difference between "hopes" and "Hope"?

Prayer: Lord Jesus, make our hope large and inclusive. Though we hope for good health and good relationships, may we focus on the great hope of eternal life.

Hope: The Land of Promises

At times we feel lost in the cosmos, pondering our identity and our destiny. Does anything make sense? Are we simply thrown into the universe without purpose or direction? Through the mystery of the Incarnation, God-made-man, our Redeemer has come among us to assure us that we are redeemed and saved. Despite the seeming absurdity of so much life and history, we trust and place our confidence in Jesus' promise of eternal life.

> In Christ, something of that other world manifests itself in the world in which we are. God, who became man, rises amongst us and says to each one of us, to me also: "I wish to redeem you from your condition of abandonment. I wish to be your salvation." To hear these words, to believe in the possibility of this promise and to trust in it despite everything inside us and around us which opposes it — this is Christian hope.
>
> (Romano Guardini)

Question: What are the things in you and around you that tempt you not to hope? How is hope connected to the promise of our redemption and salvation?

Prayer: Lord Jesus, you desire our salvation and you long to fill us with the gift of eternal life. We trust in your words; we have confidence in your promises.

three

God Is Love

Love Divine, All Loves Excelling

Christian love is incarnational. In Jesus, heaven has come down to earth and has revealed the absolute love of God for all creation. It is a love that involves compassion; it is a love that is manifest in glory. God's love saves, heals, and restores. God's love endures and surpasses our created affection.

> *Love divine, all loves excelling, Joy of heav'n to earth come down!*
> *Fix in us your humble dwelling; All your faithful mercies crown.*
> *Jesus, source of all compassion, Love unbounded love all pure;*
> *Visit us with your salvation, Let your love in us endure.*
> *Come, almighty to deliver; Let us all your life receive;*
> *Suddenly return and never, Nevermore your temples leave.*
> *Lord, we would be always blessing, Serve you as your hosts above,*

Pray, and praise you without ceasing, Glory
  in your precious love.
Finish then your new creation, Pure and
  spotless, gracious Lord;
Let us see your great salvation, Perfectly in
  you restored.
Changed from glory into glory, Till in heav'n
  we take our place,
Till we sing before the Almighty, Lost in
  wonder, love and praise.
                                    (Charles Wesley)

Question: How can God's love endure in us
moody and intemperate creatures? In what sense
is divine love related to the experience of glory?

Prayer: Lord Jesus, you came among us to
reveal the universality and extravagance of your
Father's love. Open our hearts to your divine
affection; give the courage to share your love
with all we meet.

2 God Is Love

Ever since reading how George Herbert's "Love" transformed the life of Simone Weil, I have attempted to recite and pray this poem with intense focus. Weil, suffering during a Holy Week from a painful headache, was given this poem. While reciting it over and over again, God came into her life and transformed her soul. Here is a God who is quick-ey'd Love, an initiator of friendship, and a challenging Deity who is always our divine Host. What blocks the reception of this hospitality is our narcissism, our concern about our sinful past, our unworthiness, and/or our marring of our soul and senses. God will have none of it. We must sit at the Eucharistic table and be nourished by Love and Mercy, by the mystery of God.

Is this good news too good to be true? Does God daily invite us into the divine presence, take us by the hand, smile upon us? So often the "preached" God is disappointed and wrathful, hypersensitive and full of vengeance. Not here. Not in Herbert's experience of a God known by another poet as "this tremendous Lover." Francis Thompson and George Herbert apparently sat at the same table and came to know the same God.

Love (III)

Love bade me welcome: yet my soul drew
  back, Guilty of dust and sin.
But quick-ey'd Love, observing me grow slack
From my first entrance in,
Drew nearer to me, sweetly questioning,
If I lack'd anything.

A guest, I answer'd, worthy to be here:
Love said, You shall be he.
I the unkind, ungrateful? Ah my dear,
I cannot look on thee.
Love took my hand, and smiling did reply,
Who made the eyes but I?

Truth Lord, but I have marr'd them: let my
  shame Go where it doth deserve.
And know you not, says Love, who bore the
  blame?
My dear, then I will serve.
You must sit down, says Love, and taste my
  meat: So I did sit and eat.

(George Herbert)

Question: Is your God "quick-ey'd" and "smiling"?

Prayer: Lord Jesus, you reveal to us the mystery of God, a God of compassion, love, and mercy. You reveal to us a God who is love. We praise you for such a revelation.

3 God's Spirit: Listening & Loving

Only two things are required of us in the end: to listen and to love, that is, to hear and respond, and we do that by being obedient and self-giving. By so doing, we live with and in the Spirit of the living God. But, for all our good intentions, this is no easy task. Deafness alienates us from truth; selfishness and indifference distance us from charity. Thus, too often, we live in darkness and not the light of Christ. Peace does not come to our house, as we are trapped in doing our own will. For us to change, our daily prayer must be, "Come, Holy Spirit, come!"

The art of living is mysterious and demanding. Can it be this simple (and difficult) as just listening and loving? Is all of life essentially a response to the thousand and one stimuli that come our way (and let us remember that even the initiatives we take ultimately are also a response to the proddings of our God)? The Pentecost event is paramount; without the gift of the Spirit, we shall never hear nor love as deeply as we can.

To Live with the Spirit

To live with the Spirit of God is to be a listener.
It is to keep the vigil of mystery,
earthless and still.
One leans to catch the stirring of the Spirit,
strange as the wind's will.

The soul that walks where the wind of the
                                   Spirit blows
turns like a wandering weather-vane toward love.
It may lament like Job or Jeremiah,
echo the wounded hart, the mateless dove.
It may rejoice in spaciousness of meadow
that emulates the freedom of the sky.
Always it walks in waylessness, unknowing;
it has cast down forever from its hand
the compass of the whither and the why.

To live with the Spirit of God is to be a lover.
It is becoming love, and like to Him
toward Whom we strain with metaphors of
                                   creatures:
fire-sweep and water-rush and the wind's whim.
The soul is all activity, all silence;
and though it surges Godward to its goal,
it holds, as moving earth holds sleeping
                                   noonday,
the peace that is the listening of the soul.

                                   (Jessica Powers)

Question: How well do you listen? How well
do you love?

Prayer: Lord Jesus, send your Spirit into our
hearts. May we hear and obey your word. May
we emulate you in your self-giving love.

4 Loving God for God's Sake

What's in it for me? Self-interest is deeply engrained in the human spirit. This radical tendency infects our faith as well. Do we love God for who God is or what gain we might achieve in our self-sacrifice? And how do we humbly admit that our motives are mixed and are in need of constant purification? All our efforts will ultimately fail unless we seek God's grace to love Him as we should.

> The Christian tradition in its vital years picked up something of this sense of the love of God and of trust in the divine ways wherever they lead. From the tradition of Bernard of Clairvaux in the Middle Ages there survives the story of a woman seen in a vision. She was carrying a pitcher and a torch. Why these? With the pitcher she would quench the fires of hell, and with the torch she would burn the pleasures of heaven. After these were gone, people would be able to love God for God's sake. Here, as so often in Hebrew thought, a regard for the intrinsic character of God and of divine trustworthiness shines through. A

believer shifts away from a bartering concept in which one loves God for the sake of trans-action. Now there is a relation in which the trusting one is simply reposed in the divine will. The journey through the season after solstice in the heart will take on purpose and become bearable.

(Martin Marty)

Question: Why do we love God? Is it for self-ish gain or simply because God is lovable and good?

Prayer: Lord Jesus, purify our motives. Help us to see God's glory and to respond in adoring love.

5 A Loving Prayer

Prayer is that intimate, serious conversation between God and the soul. Each of us has our own style; each of us has our own unique relationship with the Lord. One of the basic principles of prayer is to enter into that mutual dialogue with God with "who you are," warts and all. Bring into the divine presence what is on your mind and heart. Then be ready to hear what is on God's mind and heart. In that unique sharing, powerful things will happen.

"Oh, Lord," he prayed, "I put myself in Your hands. Without You I am no better than a crow, going nowhere. Without You I am alone, no more than smoke rising through the chimney and disappearing in the air. You know my situation. I put myself in Your hands, Father. Amen."

His body relaxed and he sat up straighter. He liked talking to God better than anything in the world. Before he went to sleep at night, he knelt beside the bed and prayed, and sometimes awoke the next morning to find that he'd fallen asleep on his knees. He told

God everything — about not burying Poppa on the hillside and feeling guilty for thinking that Poppa didn't deserve to be buried there, about Momma not wanting to live and how she sat in her room rocking back and forth and when he brought her supper she called him Charles and tried to kiss him like she had Poppa. Mostly when Joshua prayed, however, he told God how much he loved Him. Sometimes he just quoted verses from the psalms he'd memorized.

(Julius Lester)

Question: How do you pray? Does your prayer have the intimacy and warmth that Joshua's prayer has?

Prayer: Lord Jesus, draw us deeply into your presence. Help us to be honest and direct in our prayer.

6 The Humility & Sweetness of God

The purpose of the Church is to foster union with God and unity among ourselves. Through the sacraments and scripture, the mission is furthered. And through the great mystics of the Church, like John of the Cross and Teresa of Avila, we are given a portrait of the interior union between God and the human soul. The mystics remind us again and again that our active ministry must be balanced with a contemplative heart.

> In this interior union God communicates Himself to the soul with such genuine love that no mother's affection, in which she tenderly caresses her child, nor brother's love, nor friendship is comparable to it. The tenderness and truth of love by which the immense Father favors and exalts this humble and loving soul reaches such a degree — O wonderful thing, worthy of all our awe and admiration — that the Father Himself becomes subject to her for her exaltation, as though He were her servant and she His lord. And He is so

solicitous in favoring her as He would be if he
were her slave and she His god. So profound
is the humility and sweetness of God!

(John of the Cross)

Question: Does the father in the parable of the Prodigal Son resemble the God described above? How does John of the Cross's experience of God compare with yours?

Prayer: Lord Jesus, open our minds and hearts so that we might understand and experience the extravagance of your Father's love. Make our souls humble and loving so that we might be open to the gift of your Spirit.

7 The Urgency of Love

In attempting to describe the mystery of the Trinity, Saint Augustine uses the categories of Lover, Beloved, and Loving. No language system can adequately define the mystery of the Deity, but Augustine comes as close as anyone. God the Father is a Lover, Jesus is the Beloved of the Father, and the Loving between them speaks of the Holy Spirit. For Augustine the experience of the triune God was not some remote, esoteric, intellectual game. In his *Confessions* we hear a profound regret that for so many years this loving God was neither known nor loved by Augustine. His regret could well be ours.

> *Late have I loved you, Beauty so ancient and so new, late have I loved you! Lo, you were within, but I outside, seeking there for you, and upon the shapely things you have made I rushed headlong, I, misshapen. You were with me, but I was not with you. They held me back far from you, those things which would have no being were they not in you. You called, shouted, broke through my deaf-*

ness; you flared, blazed, banished my blind-
ness; you lavished your fragrance, I gasped,
and now I pant for you; I tasted you, and I
hunger and thirst; you touched me, and I
burned for your peace.

(Saint Augustine)

Question: Is Augustine's experience of God in any way similar to your own?

Prayer: Lord Jesus, do not let our love be too late. May we now turn to you, our loving Redeemer, with all our affection and commit ourselves to being agents of your love.

Path
of Perfection

four

Where Charity and Love Prevail

God's charity and love lies behind all the great mysteries of our faith: creation, redemption, and sanctification. Since God is Love, we must endeavor to be open to this grace and be willing to share it with others. We express God's love in a variety of ways: in the face of sin, we call it mercy; in the face of suffering, we call it compassion. All variations on a single theme: God is Love.

Where charity and love prevail,
There God is ever found;
Brought here together by Christ's love,
By love are we thus bound.

With grateful joy and holy fear,
God's charity we learn;
Let us with heart and mind and soul
Now love God in return.

Forgive us now each other's faults
As we our faults confess;
And let us love each other well
In Christian holiness.

Let strife among us be unknown,
Let all contention cease;
Be God's the glory that we seek,
Be ours God's holy peace.

Let us recall that in our midst
Dwells God's begotten Son;
As members of his body joined,
We are in Christ made one.

No race nor creed can love exclude,
If honored be God's name;
Our family embraces all
Whose Father is the same.
(Ubi Caritas, 9th century)

Question: What is the difference between the statement "God is Love" and "Love is God"? In what sense does Christ's love hold us together?

Prayer: Lord Jesus, you are the manifestation of the Father's love. May we experience your extravagant love and share it with others.

2 Bearing the Beams of Love

The search for meaning is universal. What is this life all about? According to one poet, William Blake, we are here for a short time to be loved. Bearing the beams of God's love then imposes a demand: we share that love with others. Meaning? Being loved and loving! It's as simple and as difficult as that.

The Little Black Boy

My mother bore me in the southern wild,
And I am black, but O! my soul is white;
White as an angel is the English child,
But I am black, as if bereav'd of light.

My mother taught me underneath a tree
And sitting down before the heat of day,
She took me on her lap and kissed me,
And, pointing to the east, began to say:

Look on the rising sun: there God does live
And gives his light, and gives his heat away.
And flowers and trees and beasts and men
*   receive*
Comfort in morning joy in the noonday.

And we are put on earth a little space,
That we may learn to bear the beams of love,
And these black bodies and this sunburnt face
Is but a cloud, and like a shady grove.

For when our souls have learn'd the heat to
*   bear,*
The cloud will vanish; we shall hear his voice,
Saying: come out from the grove, my love
*   and care,*
And round my golden tent like lambs rejoice.

Thus did my mother say and kissed me,
And thus I say to little English boy.
When I from black and he from white cloud
*   free,*
And round the tent of God like lambs we joy:

I'll shade him from the heat, till he can bear
To lean in joy upon our fathers knee;
And then I'll stand and stroke his silver hair,
And be like him, and he will then love me.
                                   (William Blake)

Question: What is your philosophy of life? Are we here on earth to love and to be loved?

Prayer: Lord Jesus, you came to bring us the fullness of life. It is a life of love and self-giving. May we bear the beams of your love and share them with all we meet.

3 Love's Austere Offices

We in the Northern Hemisphere know much of winter. Its brutal rawness and unrelenting unfriendliness. We who live in family systems know much about ingratitude and take for granted the duties rendered in meals and laundry, in providing shelter and shining shoes. Or, do we? Do we really understand that, as Graham Greene writes, love and responsibility are indistinguishable?

There are, in this poem, some sad autobiographical memories. As a sullen teenager and as a sophomoric university student, I spoke to my father — he who reared me and fed me and educated me — in tones wanting in gratitude and respect. I knew little then (and now) of love's austere offices, of love's lonely duties. Whenever I recite this poem, I repent.

Those Winter Sundays

Sundays too my father got up early
and put his clothes on in the blueblack cold,
then with cracked hands that ached
from labor in the weekday weather made
banked fires blaze. No one ever thanked him.

I'd wake and hear the cold splintering,
    breaking.
When the rooms were warm, he'd call,
and slowly I would rise and dress,
fearing the chronic angers of that house,

Speaking indifferently to him,
who had driven out the cold
and polished my good shoes as well.
What did I know, what did I know
of love's austere and lonely offices?

(Robert Hayden)

Question: How have you responded to the sacrifices made by your elders?

Prayer: Lord Jesus, forgive us our ingratitude. Heal us of our self-righteousness and insensitivity.

4 Love: The Great Enlarger

Love both enlarges and refines our world. Narcissism, that excessive pre-occupation with self, restricts, constrains, and confines our lives. That's why all the talk about "the road less traveled" is so popular. That less traveled road is one of love and selflessness. It is, indeed, that path that makes all the difference, not only to oneself, but to everyone else in our circle. Love contains the seeds of universality and inclusiveness. It is a big reality, as big as God since God is Love. You cannot get much larger or more refined than being Godlike.

> Love is one of the great enlargers of the person because it requires us to "take in" the stranger and to understand him, and to exercise restraint and tolerance as well as imagination to make the relationship work. If love includes passion, it is more explosive and dangerous and forces us to go deeper.
>
> (May Sarton)

Again and again his vision was interrupted by wonder at the strength of his own feeling, at the strength and sweetness of his new love — almost like the wonder a man feels at the added power he finds in himself for an art which he had laid aside for a space. How is it that the poets have said so many fine things about our first love, so few about our later love?

(George Eliot)

Question: How large and inclusive is your world?

Prayer: Lord Jesus, enlarge our worlds. Plant the grace of your love deep within our souls so that we may take in the stranger and, by so doing, take in you.

5 Loving Your Neighbor

Love demands action. Love reaches out to others despite negative feelings or no feelings at all. The lover perceives what the beloved can be and encourages his/her growth. Even in the face of obstacles and rejection, authentic love is not paralyzed. All that matters is that others might become what they were meant to be.

> Do not waste time bothering whether you "love" your neighbor; act as if you did. As soon as we do this we find one of the great secrets. When you are behaving as if you loved someone, you will probably come to love him.
>
> (C. S. Lewis)

> Among its many aspects, love is an affirmation of that which is felt as real but cannot be seen. When the tulip has grown, one can admire its beauty; but that admiration is not love. He who feels the beauty of the tulip while it is still in the bulb covered by snow

has love for the tulip. So also does one human being have love for his fellow man when he affirms the seed of potentiality in him even while it is covered over by the snows of emotional disturbance and stress.

(Ira Progoff)

Question: What is the real test that we love others? In what sense is love more about conviction than it is about emotions?

Prayer: Lord Jesus, you saw in your weak disciples the potential of great courage. Your love for them and for us gives hope. May we love as you did. May we be for others the way you were.

6 Genuine Love: Far Beyond Logic

Unless we do it ourselves, the task will not be accomplished. Our ingrained self-reliance puts us in an impossible situation. Our vocation is a call to holiness, that is, the perfection of love. But we simply cannot shed the radical narcissism that infects our very being and prevents us from being for others as we should. We can love others and our God only with the help of grace. Being put into this indebted position makes us uncomfortable. But such is our human condition. The sooner we face this reality with humility, the more quickly can we surrender ourselves to the power and graciousness of God's loving Spirit.

> *Genuine love of neighbor is impossible through human strength alone; it necessitates something new which comes from God which surpasses the logic of mere human differentiation or unification: the love of the Holy Spirit among men. Christian love does not attempt to fuse the I and the you, or to impose upon them an attitude of selflessness*

that would annihilate the individual. It is the disposition of reciprocal openness and autonomy together, that simultaneous intimacy and dignity which comes from the Holy Ghost.
(Romano Guardini)

Question: Why is it that we cannot, by our own strength and will power, love others as God would have us love?

Prayer: Lord Jesus, when you appeared to the frightened disciples, you breathed on them and gave your peace and the gift of the Holy Spirit. Breathe on us now. May your Holy Spirit empower us to love as you love.

7
Love:
The Path to
Perfection

What or who is it that will bring us happiness? Our thirst for fullness of being lies in the direction of knowledge and love. Things, stuff, finite pleasure all fail to satisfy our infinite longings. Conventional wisdom pushes us toward power and pleasure, prestige and possessions. In the end, we remain empty and restless. Only love, love of God and our neighbors, puts us on the road to happiness and perfection.

> Service meant at best the material amelioration of the lot of man; the metaphysical tradition has been lost. Christianity, like the nineteenth century, believed in progress; believed in the search for happiness and perfection; believed therefore that it was the destiny of man to achieve the perfection of his personality on every level of life. But it believed that that process of perfection must be subsumed under a deeper, and at first sight, paradoxical, quest: the quest for self-loss in God. The creature is perfect only when his proper perfection is

subordinated to his creaturely relationship with the Creator. It is not a question of ethical unselfishness; it is far deeper than that. It is simply the deepest and irrefragable of all human facts: that life is not life unless it is love, and that love consists essentially not in getting but in giving; and primarily, giving not material things but the spirit, the self. Only by self-love in the Infinite is the thirst for the Infinite quenched; and when that is denied to man he will look for other objects in the finite world and, since they are finite, they will not suffice. Hence restlessness, confusion, pessimism; and it is to these things and not to the peace that surpasseth understanding that nineteenth-century optimism has led us. For nothing could be more alien to an anthropocentric world, convinced that nothing existed except what science could apprehend and explain, than the notion of such a metaphysical emptying of selfhood.

(Gerald Vann)

Question: Why is it that love alone can slack our thirst and satisfy our hunger?

Prayer: Lord Jesus, you have taught us, by your self-giving love, the path to happiness. Empower us through your Spirit to imitate your self-emptying love. Without your grace, we will be eternally restless.

Sources

P. 11: Melody: Gott Sei Dank 77.77 Music: Freylinghausen's Gesangbuch, 1704. Text: Le Mans Breviary, 1748. Translator: Henry W. Baker, 1821-1877.

P. 13: George Herbert: *The Country Parson, The Temple,* edited, with an introduction by John N. Wall, Jr. (New York: Paulist Press, 1981), p.178.

P. 15: *Selected Poetry of Jessica Powers,* edited by Regina Siegfried, ASC, and Robert F. Morneau (Washington, DC: ICS Publications, 1999), p. 197. All copyrights, Carmelite Monastery, Pewaukee, WI. Used with permission.

P. 16: G. K. Chesterton, *The Everlasting Man* (New York: A Doubleday Image Book, 1955), p. 243.

P. 17: Romano Guardini, *The Life of Faith,* translated by John Chapin (Westminster, Maryland: The Newman Press, 1961).

P. 18: *Letters of Flannery O'Connor: The Habit of Being,* selected and edited by Sally Fitzgerald (New York: Farrar, Strauss, Giroux, 1979).

P. 20: Romano Guardini, *The Life of Faith,* translated by John Chapin (Westminster, Maryland: The Newman Press, 1961).

P. 22: Avery Dulles, S.J., *The Assurance of Things Hoped For* (New York: Oxford University Press, 1994).

P. 27: John Newton, 1725-1807; *A Collection of Sacred Ballads,* 1790. Music: New Britain; Columbian Harmony, 1829.

P. 28: Edgar Allan Poe, *Complete Poems* (New York: Gramercy Books, 1992), p. 128.

P. 30: Anne Porter, *An Altogether Different Language: Poems 1934-1994* (Cambridge, Massachusetts: Zoland Books, 1994), p. 10.

P. 32: Flannery O'Connor, *Mystery and Manners,* Occasional Prose, selected & edited by Sally and Robert Fitzgerald (New York: Farrar, Strauss & Giroux, 1957), p. 78.

P. 33: Mircea Eliade, *Ordeal by Labyrinth: Conversations with Claude-Henri Rocquet,* translated by Derek Coltman (Chicago: The University of Chicago Press, 1982), p. 78.

P. 35: John Macquarrie, *Christian Hope* (Seabury Press, 1975), p. 106.

P. 37: Romano Guardini, *The Life of Faith,* translated by John Chapin (Westminster, MD: The Newman Press, 1961), p. 70.

P. 40: Text: 87; Charles Wesley, 1707-1788, alt. Music: HYFRYDOL; Rowland H. Prichard, 1811-1887.

P. 43: George Herbert: *The Country Parson, The Temple,* edited, with an introduction by John N. Wall, Jr. (New York: Paulist Press, 1981), p. 316.

P. 45: *Selected Poetry of Jessica Powers*, edited by Regina Siegfried, ASC, and Robert F. Morneau (Washington, DC: ICS Publications, 1999), p. 197. All copyrights, Carmelite Monastery, Pewaukee, WI. Used with permission.

P. 46: *A Cry of Absence: Reflections for the Winter of the Heart* by Martin E. Marty and illustrated by Susan Teumer Marty. Text ©1983 Martin E. Marty. Illustrations © 1983 Susan Teumer Marty. Reprinted by permission of HarperCollins Publishers (San Francisco: HarperCollins Publishers, 1983), p. 60.

P. 48: Julius Lester, *Do Lord Remember Me* (New York: Holt, Rinehart and Winston, 1984), p. 46.

P. 50: *The Collected Works of St. John of the Cross*, translated by Kieran Kavanaugh, O.C.D., and Otilio Rodriguez, O.C.D. (Washington, D.C.: ICS Publications, Institute of Carmelite Studies, 1973), p. 517.

P. 52: *The Confessions of St. Augustine*, translated by Maria Boulding O.S.B., Book 10, Chapter 27 (New York: New City Press, 1997).

P. 56: Text: CM; Ubi Caritas, 9th century; translated by Omer Westendorf, 1916-1997. Music: CHRISTIAN LOVE; Paul Benoit, OSB, 1893-1979. Text and music © 1960, World Library Publications. All rights reserved.

P. 58: *The Complete Poetry and Prose of William Blake*, edited by David V. Erdman (Berkeley: University of California Press, 1982), p. 9.

P. 61: Robert Hayden, *Collected Poems* (October House, 1966).

P. 62: May Sarton, *Journal of a Solitude* (New York: W. W. Norton & Company, 1973), p. 93.

P. 63: George Eliot, *Adam Bede* (New York: New American Library, 1981), p. 475.

P. 64: C. S. Lewis, *Mere Christianity* (New York: Macmillan Company, 1946), 116.

P. 65: Ira Progoff, *The Symbolic & the Real* (New York: McGraw-Hill Book Company, 1963), p. 62.

P. 66: Romano Guardini, *The Lord* (Chicago, Henry Regnery Company, 1954), p. 434.

P. 68: Gerald Vann, *St. Thomas Aquinas* (Chicago: Benziger Brothers, 1940), pp. 25-26.